A Vessel
Born to Float

Andrews McMeel Publishing
a division of Andrews McMeel Universal
1130 Walnut Street, Kansas City, Missouri 64106

www.andrewsmcmeel.com

24 25 26 27 28 TEN 10 9 8 7 6 5 4 3 2 1

ISBN: 978-1-5248-9256-2

Library of Congress Control Number: 2024933927

Editor: Danys Mares
Art Director/Designer: Tiffany Meairs
Production Editor: Jasmine Lim
Production Manager: Alex Alfano

Cover design by Lori Saint Rome

ATTENTION: SCHOOLS AND BUSINESSES

Andrews McMeel books are available at quantity discounts with bulk purchase for educational, business, or sales promotional use. For information, please e-mail the Andrews McMeel Publishing Special Sales Department: sales@amuniversal.com.

A Vessel
Born to Float

Poems

Yazmin Monét Watkins

Andrews McMeel
PUBLISHING®

No matter how hard we try to ignore it, the mind always knows truth and wants clarity.

—Toni Morrison, *God Help the Child*

For us. I see you sis.

Contents

I

Expanding

Too Much

I don't want no more sadness
You can go on and take it with you
Pack it up, you enjoy it
Box it up, bring it back to your home
I don't want
No more sorrow at my door
I barely got enough joy to keep my damn self afloat
Can't you see I'm already over here scooping sadness by the spoonful?
Please go on somewhere else with your sorrow
I ain't got no more room for tears
Go on and keep
Your sorry-ass politicians with their Band-Aid solutions
Y'all want to maintain the status quo so bad
Y'all can go on and hold on to that somewhere else
Go on and keep your viral videos
Your public lynching picnic pics
I promise, I promise I got enough right here
I done got so much grief piled up at my door
I can't even get past my front lawn
Can't make it past one post, past the overwhelm
Can't make it past the gauntlet of group chats grinding to a halt yet again
Someone, anybody, sing me a joyful tune
A righteous resistance and revival
Sing me the song of our triumph and soon come freedom
Sing me the signal and end of state-sanctioned violence against our people
Come sing me the song of organizers in the street, power in our feet
Sing me the song where this time
We don't settle, we win.
What are you doing, fam?
What are you doing with this one life we've got?
What are you giving right now to make it right?
I don't want no more sadness
I promise I got enough right here.
I'm tryna fight, I'm tryna win.
I can't let you drag me down with you
We got too much to do
So much life yet to live.

Strange Garden

I am in bed with my man
Glorious that he be
I could use a sip of water
Perhaps the whole bottle
In truth I could really go for some gin
Mix it with Lillet and rose
Call it a strange garden.

Hot damn, I am parched
It is the heat of summer
I need a drink of water.
Did I mention
I'm getting married
By the sea?
I am in love and full of salt.
Bloated. Come to my river
Wash my soul.

Do other bi folks ever think these thoughts?
Do they have their Sprinkles cupcakes
And eat them too?

Hello, world, am I all alone?
I should be sleeping.
Instead I'm dreaming of cocktails and pastries.

The waitress asks, do I want breakfast or lunch?
Every time we brunch, I falter.
Savory or sweet?
I usually ask for both.

The White Ally Wants to Know How to Bridge Movements (Across Race, Gender, and Sexuality)

As if there were any way to unbraid these identities
Plaited through my spine

Nappy-curled and thick.
As if I did not emerge from my mother's womb

Slick with the bloody history
Of bending over backwards to help you

Understand. As though I am not
Already inherently a bridge.

As if my back is not the shining
scar-plated plank you traverse

To understanding.
Understand, I am tired

Of reaching out to closed fists,
Of trying to be friendly, to smile,

To curtail this rightful rage.
You want to know how to work together?
Listen.

Mortality

If today is the day death will come
His bony arm outstretched

Will he snatch me under that billowing cape
on the dark, lonely drive home?

Wheels skidding into the side of the guardrail
in a mess of fiery disaster

Or perhaps my plane will take flight
And never land in one whole piece

Some freak accident
Will find me spiraling down the shaft of a broken elevator
Just a few stops to an untimely death

Will my face appear on the day's local news tragedies?
Some Facebook clickbait or yet another hashtag

Gunned down by the police
while I was out running

I think about death
seeing all those he has taken

Without rhyme or care
For time or place
Need or space

Not asking if I was ready to go
I am sure he will show me the same courtesy
as those who have gone before me

They say we do not know the day nor the hour
I wonder what happens to our souls
when we cross that great gold threshold

What will I find on the other side?

So many have already boarded that train
The one thing I know
Without a question of doubt
Is that I will die

Hopefully so much later than soon come
I pray that I will be given time

There is so much I have yet to do.

Borrowed Tongue

I speak with a borrowed tongue
In the language of an oppressor
English does not feel like a place to call home.

I imagine all the possible dialects I could have come from
And try on Creole. Try on Yoruba.
Like a young girl in her mother's clothes
Too big, too complicated
More fabric woven into all my flags
Than I know what to do with.

I don't fully understand why
English feels like a foreign language
When this is all I know of *nation*
My race, class, gender, and sexuality
All reminders of why I am more second-class
Than citizen

Born in a country where my children
Are not safe from unchecked fear
Tossed in tumultuous tempers
Feeling anything but

Home
I wear this red, white, and blue with trepidation
A wary outsider within
A complicated history
Whispers of forgotten stories

An erased visibility.
More question mark
Than origin tale
I know nowhere is perfect.

But all I've got for background
Is my grandparents' light skin
Expressing itself in my own

Hailing from the South without much collective memory
Our family has no crest
No tidy explanation of our generations
Just blank roots dangling from our family tree

Wondering
Who was my grandmother's mother
And her mother's mothers before them?

From what branch were they plucked?
What languages did they leave back home?

Where did they learn to speak?
Sorry (not sorry), *plantation* ain't good enough

I wonder what my voice would sound like
Without the erasure
Without the colonization

Sometimes I dream of
Flying to countries
Even my ancestors wouldn't recall
A space where our true song and dance
Drums deep in our speech pattern
The floral rhythm of rolling *r*'s
Full of mango and spice

I am an orphan
Robbed from a language
I will never get to move into

I wish I knew where my blood came from.

Perhaps that is the root
Of my irresistible urge to travel
Wander lusting in my bones
Always searching for some place
To finally call home.

For My Grandmother Lillie

Family holidays at the Bartlow (Watkins) residence are usually spent bonding around my mother's cooking, a tradition started by my grandmother's birthday and grandiose Christmas celebrations. We all gathered around my mother's candied yams, collard greens, stuffing made with real cornbread and celery. My favorite dish is her world-famous macaroni and cheese. (Famous around the world mostly because I talk about it everywhere I go—trust me, it's bomb.)

As we were going through the photos Cousin Paul had brought over of my mother's Aunt Rosa, as we were looking at my Great-Grandmother Turney (who I was seeing for the first time in photograph), we got to my grandmother.

Impeccably dressed. Could almost pass for white but stayed Black and proud to raise three Black and proud children who would one day raise this Black and proud woman.

The one and only Lillie Velma Turney.

A flood of questions coursed through me: What were my grandmother and her sister's lives like? What did they do for a living? What did they do for fun? What lessons could they teach me today? What warnings could they give me about bearing this Black skin in America?

I learned how we fit into the broader jigsaw puzzle of a history of these "united states."

I saw photos of my grandmother and her sister, just like my sister and I. Close. Sharing hugs and smiles in velvet booths at Club Alabam, Joe Morris's Plantation Club, Slim Jenkins Cafe. In furs, in heels, in dresses I wish I had today. In front of cars from yesterday. In homes they built with tomorrow in mind.

On the arms of the likes of Jackie Robinson and my fox of a grand-father, Robert Bartlow, the Turney sisters had it goin' on back then. I wish I knew them today. Wish we could have hung out and listened to live music together.

We could swap clothes and tell stories about broken hearts and lonely nights. About betrayal, inside and outside of the home. About what it's like to be Black and fly in America. To have sisters (best friends) who live miles away but still keep in touch like no time has passed. And to have strong mothers hell-bent on making better lives for us, even if that meant sacrifice. I want them to tell me how to let the racism so deeply planted in this country wash over me like a wave and somehow keep breathing underwater.

These are scary times for Black folks (I'm not talking about the 1930s). I bet my grandmother could tell me something of race relations in the South. Of Black bodies and poplar trees. Of burning flesh that smells all too familiar today. Of tears that don't stop falling and rage that just won't stop burning. Of warning people too blinded by their own ignorance to see the house burning down all around us.

Grandma, how did you deal with the ignorance? How did you man-age to survive? I want to understand our history. I want to know more of your migration westward. Of moving homes, chasing dreams in a world that does not see you. Tell me about our history and yours. Tell me everything. I feel lost. And exhausted. And I'm so tired of running around the same conversations. This is a never-ending race in a hostile place, and justice is a finish line I'm not quite sure this country will ever reach.

But beyond all that, I wish you were here.

Grandma, tell me what it's like to bear witness to rioting in the streets and trying not to let the grief consume you whole. I look to the past for answers. My mother tells me she gets her spiritual backbone from you, and so, in turn, have I.

I try not to despair. Try to follow the brave example you set for your family and just try to enjoy this moment where we are all gathered together. I munch on mac and cheese and try to relax and reflect and welcome your spirit here with us today. I feel you, Grandma Lillie, and you communicate your answer:

Rise above.

Grandma Mabel

I don't speak often about my paternal grandmother
Of the few memories I have
I remember hot summers on her Long Beach carpet
Reading *Jet* magazine next to the fan
I remember the way she ate fried chicken at Pann's in Ladera,
My last memory of fried chicken before I gave up meat.
I see her now clearing the table
Stacking napkins and plates and bones in one pile
The way my father chastised her for doing someone else's job
I remember taking the bus with her
So proud of her ability to move on her own
I remember the nursing home in Baldwin Hills taking that away
The way her body seemed to disappear
How small she became
How little she remembered (Alzheimer's be one hell of a disease)
How guilty I felt whenever we'd go visit.

I remember most her hands
Specifically her fingers, knobby, thin, and frail
They were the most elegant fingers
I like to think I get my nails from her.
Long beds with champagne-colored sheets
Striped down the middle of a select few.
She too passed before I knew to ask questions.
From what I hear
Grandma Mabel was from Little Rock
Worked her whole life for McDonnell Douglas
She birthed my father, my two uncles
And my Aunt Yvonne, who so reminds me of her
in those final days.
I know she survived poverty and trauma
I know she divorced my grandfather early
But my father prays annually at their shared grave.
As a grown woman now
I see I am also hers
Despite whatever complications

I have not resolved with my father,
I am still hers.
I am both grateful and amazed
She too is a part of me.

Too Many Open Tabs

My iPhone tells me I have too many open tabs
Asks if I want to close the 427 older than one month
I am a bit of a digital hoarder
My mind be collecting memories like that
Packing away as many moments as I can hold
My arms too full
Trying to hold on to the good stuff:
Lyrics to Noname's "Song 33," the PDF link to my first script with
David, *Nuns with Guns,* Voluspa candles I would've bought if only they
were Black owned
All these tabs open wide, a monument to my anxiety
COVID testing sites pop up on my timeline
Surveys demanding justice,
Prove Black Lives Matter to you, Hollywood
What color is change again?
I be gettin' lost
Think of afterthoughts
Lianne La Havas croons "Paper Thin"
And somehow she knows the pain I'm in
Knows I just looked up the seven stages of Alzheimer's
Knows my Google search history reads "death of a parent and what
to expect"
Knows I just bared my soul and broke down at Norman Houston Park
There have to be alternatives to calling the police, right?
Like, surely Adult Protective Services doesn't need cops for our elders?
Can't wait to talk to my therapist about all this
I need to pay that invoice on her site
Apple Pay'll be just fine
ScorpioMystique tells me we're going through a major period of
purging
Physical and psychological debris
I let too many memories take up too much space
And what would it mean to start over?
To start fresh? What happens
When I finally close all these tabs?

La Sirène

She speaks
In ocean
La Sirène
Living
In her bones
First love
Taboo tangled
What confusion
Lust
Must move
No choice
but to grab hold.
She brings me music
Has me singing
Metrès de oseyan,
manman nan lanmè a
Magick miracle
Sun shining
Behind our kisses
I am altar
She is shrine
Light blue candle
in a crystal bowl.
She be light house
I, shipwrecked treasure
Floating diamonds and champagne
Oysters on the half shell
(She says she likes the way they taste)
Coral and pearl
Offerings
I bathe in her honeydrop
Sea salt and condensed milk
Dripping down my walls
Azul flowers in white basin
Poured slowly over body
I am rushing river

rippling to her doorstep.
Tonight we worship
The tug and stretch
The grasp and grab
She is mermaid, she is healing
Ensnares my moon with all her tide
Beloved goddess
Yemayá in different tongue
Ruling hypnotherapy
in my dreams.
She sees secrets
Holds them closely
As near as she does me.
Her ocean pulls me under
And I willingly dive.
La Sirène, La Balèn
Chapo'm tonbe nan lanmé.
The Mermaid, The Whale
My hat fell into the sea.

Her Fingers

Peel hard-boiled eggs in the sink
She pulls the shell apart the way she does me
Layer by layer, let loose
She prepares ramen, cuts onions by the sink
Shows me how to cut
I am mesmerized by her hands
Took this photo of her at the market
She plucks the most perfect produce
Mangoes, peaches, and limes
No Frank Ocean song, I am in love
And requited. She picks me.
Plucks and strums every chord
Touches me and every light turns on
A flood of joy and care and song
Oh, the way she feels
Fingers flitting cross erogenous zones
I did not even know existed
God really went to work when She crafted her fingers
Bless O the hands
That prepare this meal
Fruit-bearing fingers
Dripping nectar just as sweet
Her hand in my hand,
On my thigh, in my mouth
What a bountiful feast
A most delicious meal
The kind a tongue could savor
Well into the next lifetime.

Snacks for Drifting

I wish that I could be there right now
To kiss the coal off your eyes
To pull you in toward my body
Arms around you
Heart against your back
As you drift off for just five more
Minutes are rare with you
A delicacy, you say
I feast on the moments we get
Together, such a delicious word
Make myself full on memories
I cherish so deep
Send you poems to snack on
Until our next morning

The Magic of Luck and Love (Or Long Distance)

This period of love and play and butterflies
Hummingbirds singing sweet lullabies
Thrummed against my rib cage
My heart beating so fast in your palms
What gods smiled from above and said *play*?
What angels sung our love from the heavens?
What gods crossed our paths and said
Drink?
Bless O the trumpets that called you here to my heart
Bless O the affirmations that brought our two souls to the other
Shower me in all the green clovers
The fields of sunshine rising grand over each new day
That I get to call you mine
That I get to be yours
I am yours
My love
My most sweet and perfect dream
My love made manifest and magic
What are my days now without you?
What will they be without you?
Loving every drop of this present
I lap you up
Savoring all I can hold
Bursting at the seams
Until I feel
You in my arms again

Not Quite U-Haul (The Road Trip Home)

We drive through the southern states
Risk life and limb and Alabama PD
Cruise down Route 66 on cruise control
Drive past construction zones—slow
(God, I hate traffic)
We stumble through tough topics:
The fear, the timing, the scheduling of it all.
The reality that I (we) may not be enough
Heat blasts in the car, hot as the fire we make when we are together
Outside New Mexico, frigid as she is when she doesn't think we'll
work
It's possible
I don't know how long I can do this
My eyes water already, god.

And yet, hour seven on the road and I'm still driving
Hoping she gets even just a moment of rest
She sleeps shotgun
Holds my hand even after she's dreaming

I pray we make it.
Not even sure where "it" is
Death, tracksuits, this move to LA?
Who even knows.
For now though
Her hand is in mine.
The sky is full of wishing stars
And the road ahead is endless.

How to Break Your Own Heart:

Fall in love with
yet another
monogamous
woman.

Leftovers

Looking for love
In unavailable people
Who taught you to rummage
For leftovers? Grab 'n' go?
Who taught you to brown paper bag your feelings
Who showed you your value
(Ain't nobody listening)
Rolling up to thrift stores
In high style
Who showed you how women were to be treated
Like cars
Open doors
Polish their rims
Cherish them like children
Like girlfriends
Or wait,
An afterthought
That's more fitting
Like
I wonder who taught her
That's what love looks like
Good thing she built a thick shell
This is a slow race
Running in circles
Nothing ever changes
She's out of breath
Wheezing
Wondering when, or if
There will ever be real love

Hold up, hold up
First
Pose for the picture
Smile
You know they love that fake shit

(he don't even know what love looks like
moldy and green
cut off that growth
he don't know how messy,
how alive that shit be)

She be giving and giving
No hands to receive it
Too clumsy
Maybe that's where she gets it.
Is that where she comes from?
What happens to all that extra love?
Sitting on the fridge shelf
Wrapped up in tinfoil
What happens to all those leftovers?
Spoiling room-temp yogurt
Fermenting fruit, once sweet
Now curdled and bitter
Several years past their expiration.

Sometimes She Visits Me in My Dreams

I'll be standing there pregnant
Drinking three beers
Drunk and then I look down to see her
My belly round as a full moon
I feel her sloshing around in my adolescence
I was not ready

In my dreams I prepare to recite a poem for her
About her
How she kicked and screamed out of my body
She a sparking rocket, a spaceship exploding in the sky
Blood and vomit, excremental in her soar
I think of the doctor
Her clipped *there's no turning back now*
That knowing

In my dreams she is never actually a person
Just potential
A boulder in my belly
A poem from my lips
She is never quite here
Having never truly arrived
She is always leaving
In some shape or form
Formless
My two-week-old daughter visits me
And I feel her
Know we had a connection
However brief it may have been

Most years, these days
I can hide it
Push away her memory
Push away the kick and scream
(I did actually push her out of my body.)
Most days she is just a floating memory

A haunting premonition of joy that's yet to be
A dream already faded
When I open my eyes.

What to Expect When You Least Expect It
(On Losing Something That Was Never Yours)

You are a tornado,
busy as a whirlwind,
changing the world with a cyclone sparking in your footsteps.
However,
when you finally spin out and slow down
long enough to sit at the head of your own table,
these things you will find cobwebbed
in the spaces you tried to forget:

1.
You will see her face in every curly-haired sunshine you see passing by.
You will think none of them could ever be more sunflower brilliance
than the one you have birthed in your imagination.

2.
He will haunt your dreams with an unwanted wisp of regret whispering
deep at your core that you will never remember what it felt like before
your sorrow ever had a name: Loss, Pain, "Too Late to Turn Back
Now." How a doctor could ever say such things to a patient, you will
never understand.

3.
You will see her tragic smile in the wings of a grasshopper
struggling to free itself from a passing car
stuck in traffic in a language you can never give voice to
its will to hold on to life
will find a way to root her name in your hearth.
You will not remember what it felt like before you felt her.

4.
There will be times when you allow yourself to forget she ever
almost happened.
You will frolic on the ghost meadow of your childhood, and for a
moment

The sun, the waves, the smiles split open like jawbreakers, will spill
rainbow from your lips
Your laughter giggling from a place that almost forgot how to have fun.
It is here, floating in this sea of sorrow
Her face will capsize your rubber floatie
Swallow you under an unforgiving silence.
The past has no care for your current joy.

5.
You are entitled to your rage. It will force its way into casual conversa-
tion, an extra dinner guest uncomfortable at your side. The air thick
as the moment you discovered your white friends were actually prone
to racist tendencies.

Something red will bubble out beneath your well-manicured surface
and you will not know what to call it: anger, relief, frustration.
Storm.

Nothing makes sense.

And there, in the middle of your attempted day-to-day, business as usual,
typhoons will fire up your tongue and release thunderstorms.

Try not to get caught up in the parking, the lateness,
the misunderstanding of it all, and call it by its real name:
abortion, heartache,
the elephant in the room.
Don't panic. When the tears come (and they will),
these are signs you are still human.

6.
Funny, you will look back and discover there was a reason you went to
all those rallies.
Good thing a former incarnation of yourself
Chanted loud enough to secure your present self an option.
You will realize there is nothing funny about it.
Despite what white men in white houses have tried to take away
You had a choice, a right to own your own body

They want to save her fetus
But refuse to care for her when she gets here
No one knows you like you do
You are not a pawn in this political warfare
You are a woman
You are human
You were not ready.

7.
It's okay to not know how this poem ends.
No neat ending for your tears.
Perhaps years later you will actually know what to say.
Truthfully, there really is no way to prepare for the unthinkable.
You made the best decision for where you were at that time in your life.
Do not repress your sadness. You have permission to feel.
You have the right to grieve.

Run

Hey, Yazmin, girl
Whatchu running from?
Where you running to?
Where you going?
When you coming back?
Where you been?
What'd you see?
How'd you feel?
You feelin' okay?
You feelin' at all?
Are you even human?
Do you ever stop to rest?
You takin' care of yourself?
You takin' care now?
Takin' aim?
You shootin'?
For your dreams?
For the stars?
Hiding from your scars?
Whatchu doin'?
Where you goin'?
You ever gonna stay?
Settle down?
When you gon' quit?
Give up?
Whatchu running from?
Why you running?
Why you running?
What are you running from?

The World's Guide to Ending
after Marty McConnell

Where do we go when there are no more questions left to ask?
When we have nothing left to give,
What becomes of our silence?
Don't be afraid of the stillness
The light is actually inside of you
The darkness is only another territory to root our flag
Dig in, cross the threshold
The beginning is never complete without an end
But before you go
You spark a bullet, you
Incite a riot
Refuse to go calmly
Bare your teeth
Scrape your knuckles
Scrap and fight and kick
Don't be fooled
We only have this moment
To really claim what we deserve
Turn the world on its head
Rattle your cobra tongue
Discard everything you were told
Peel it off like new skin
Pick it off like a scab
Rip it clean, start anew.
Scar.
Blood is only a temporary obsession
Turn me on
I want to feel what's inside of you
Let's really find out what you're made of
You are gorgeous
Hideous
You freak of nature
Unravel all your insecurities
Find a reason to cry
To feel

Give in to your emotions
Falling in love is easy
Maintaining meaning is the challenge
The wheel of fortune favors the lovers
So kiss the dice
Play all your chips
Heart trumps everything
Remember
Nothing else matters
Darling, you are a dreamer
That not many understand, but
Shine, shine anyway
That is why they call so few
A constellation
The world is waiting for your brilliance
Occupy your life, while you still have it
What good is a funeral to an empty shell
Have your wake before you die
Enjoy your family here and now
Come now,
The world is going to hell in a handbasket
Of fire and brimstone anyway
Feel the ecstasy in your veins
Laugh, dance, cry, exalt
Love until your coals ember
Love until *hallelujah* sounds like coming
Praise until it sounds like dying
Till it sounds like howling
Till it sounds like struggle
Like survival
Like revival
Like Alpha
Omega
AlphaOmegaAlphaOmega
Are we the chicken or the egg?
There is no more time for questions
We only have one shot at living here

The gods are listening—now
Tell them how you really feel.

Aphrodite at the River Styx

we have arrived at the River Styx
I printed out the only two photographs
we ever had
together
and pasted them over each eyelid
offering Charon my most valuable
snapshots of our memories
our love
a real dead loving.
a pyred shrine, aching and unrequited
our ship sails bi
floating downstream with
the pieces of me that once
burned
for you.
ashes to ashes
dust to fire
such is the nature of life.
there are sand storms
licking in my larynx now
dry and creaking
nothing lasts forever
this love is no exception.
this poem is all the fare I have
is all the air I need
to wade underwater
and finally let go.

II

Crashing

9 Things I Really Meant to Say to the White Boy Who Thought It Was Okay to Shove His Hands in My Hair Last Night at the Bar after I Politely Said Don't Do It:

1.

Not sure why you haven't learned this basic concept already
But for your first lesson
In acceptable social behavior:
DON'T. PUT. YOUR. HANDS. IN. MY. HAIR.
I do not know you.
There is no reason I should feel
Your grubby fingertips
On my scalp.
Ever.
Don't do it.

2.

I get it.
My hair is amazing. Yeah, I know.
You've never seen anything like it.
Maybe you don't have any Black friends back home
Who could have warned you, but—
Don't touch a Black girl's hair.
I am not your Chia Pet.
My hair not some pampered poodle
My body not a petting zoo
For your personal perusal.
Paws off.

3.

You just fucked up my curl pattern, man!
Do you know how much
Coconut curl creme I had to use
To tame this fro?

That stuff is not cheap!

4.
In what world
Is it ever acceptable
To touch strangers
Without permission?

Is there some reason
You felt welcome
To invade my section of the bar
With your neocolonialist exploration
And lay your hands on my person?

I am not your property.

Stop looking like I kicked your kitten
By telling you
You don't have the right to grope me.

5.
If you truly have questions about Black hair
And its care
There's this amazing World Wide Web of resources called
The internet.

Look it up.

6.
Real talk,
Why is it always white people
Who feel so privileged to reach right on in?

Who taught you that our
Bodies were yours
For the touching?

For the taking?

Who taught you that
Consent does not matter?

I don't care how curious you are
Your primitive interest
In a cultural exploration of "other"
Does not trump my discomfort.

7.
While we're at it
When was the last time
You walked up to a white woman
And fondled her hair?

What makes you feel so entitled
To violate my personal space?
I was trying to be nice, but

8.
Fuck I look like?
This is not some 1800s exhibition
I am not on display.
Furthermore,
I don't know you like that.
I'm sitting here like everyone else
Trying to enjoy my passion fruit margarita
As I was peacefully doing before you came along
And shoved your hands deep inside me.

9.
Did you forget that it's the twenty-first century?
I don't owe you an explanation.
My body, my hair, my space
Period.
Unless I explicitly give you permission.

For the last time, dude,

Look, But Don't Touch.

Sisterhood of the Curly Cartel

Somewhere in America
Perhaps at this very moment
A curl is dying.

Every hydrated ounce is
Pressed
Burned
Sometimes held hostage.

We launch chemical warfare
On the vibrance of our spirit.
Under the bitter dictate
of the hot-iron thumb,

Brown girls take iron to hand
Hand to fist
Heat to hair and
Make tresses play a cacophony
of sounds that string flat.

Teased into philharmonic "perfection".
We spend hours
Attacking our goddess-given coils
With hot oils and sprays

Fighting the parts of ourselves
Locked into the fiber
Of our aftershocked core.

We press and curl
Our naturals
Ignoring DNA's intention
Losing all the storied magic curled into just one strand
Kinky, quirky, coily, beautiful.

Convinced of foreign standards
We forget our natural hair
Is more miracle than mishap
More marvelous than mortified
More monarch than monster.
Rockin' a crown atop our heads

We move from straight-laced margin
To curled and proud center.

We are born of a tradition
Of natural-haired women warriors
Fist in the air, pen on the pad, curls in the breeze
So stop cowering from moisture
And baptize your strands in self-love.
Our hair has been made slave
To the hot-iron dictate for too long.

The grass is greenest where you water it
And moisturize with curly pudding
So break those straight shackles
And bounce freely, dear curls.

Proudly rock that garland of good hair
And this ringlet wreath of freedom
Gather 'round, dear sisters
The truth no longer secret
The sisterhood of the curly cartel
Has now been called to order.

The Selfie

a LACMA commission for The Obama Portraits Tour

We gather to selfie with our favorite president
Snapping photographic memories of extraordinary
humans we almost know
Can almost touch
Here to witness the grandeur of Black excellence
Gazing back at us at eye level
Larger than life and still
complex, complicated,
Our President and First Lady
(The only ones we acknowledge)
Trailblazers for configuration
Bathed in fields of green and blue
Black and white against color
A reframed reverence and respect
Here they can do no wrong
We lay flowers at their feet
Chrysanthemums and jasmine
African blue lilies and geometric patterns
Quilted idealizations of the past
We say both hello and farewell
Remembering a time when we thought
Anything was possible
And that change was a price we could afford
Hope, as bright as Election Day
We treasure the remembrance
Tiny ties of the threads that lead to theirs
The part we all played
knocking door to door
canvassing his campaign in college
My first lesson in civic engagement
And even though we don't always agree
about snappy slogans and defunding the police
Mom and Dad did raise us to get involved
Jokingly called him father
Obama's Other Daughters

Brought his cardboard cutout to every single show

Tell me you in a Black home without telling me you in a Black home
I remember visits to my godmother's house in Inglewood
The only figures on display:
Black Jesus and Obama's inauguration smile
Framed on front-page paper
And a statue of Michelle, an icon of Black womanhood
More homegirl than distant royal
They have always been a part of the family

He reminds me of my father after an infinite day of work
Unbuttoned, unbothered, finally at rest

Family back home for the holidays from DC
Here to sit with us for a spell
A seat at a table we once served
Come to find us here at home from
Chicago, to Brooklyn, to Los Angeles, Houston, and Atlanta

An ode to Black love in practice
A paraded paint and pitchfork
We know them to be ours
Symbols of hope and potential
The reality of what is and was
Gorgeous and inherently human
Made to love us back

On the Day of Yet Another Mass Shooting

Carpe diem
Seize the day, or
More literally
Pick or pluck
Enjoy, seize, use
That good ole American way—
Business as usual
Pluck the day [as it is ripe]

O say, how we pluck
Like chicken feathers
Ripe, with blood at the root
What an Anglo tradition
To seize
To take
What a righteous red, white, and blue
To pick what is not ours
A life
And claim it as our own.

Over There

It is 12:13 on my midnight flight from Philly
I sing an oldie-but-goodie in my head
And wake to
Lightning across the way
Igniting the dark clouds
With atomic fire

Zeus, with all his mighty thunder,
Throws stabs of light across the sky
Focused on just this one city
I wonder who lives beneath
Behind me, seat 16F pulls out her phone
Records the pixelated light show
Then goes back to reading *Time* magazine

I say to myself, *thank God the storm is over
there*. Flying through perfect white
quiet, I say, *damn, look over there
How fucked up it must be
for the persons living underneath
that wild strike of violence*

I crane my neck
Looking for the blinking light of city below
Knowing there is nothing I can do
But pray
Knowing that prayer without action
Is never enough

Miracle

We find our rhythm
Six hands in tandem
Tucking, folding, wiping the day clean
Tina turns and applies the cream
Jade rubs her head
I lotion her shins and feet
We bathe her and get her ready
Tucked softly into bed
Surrounded by love and care
She starts to slumber
It is an honor to care for my mother
Tender, like all the love poured into me
I stroke her head until she falls asleep
Whisper affirmations cross her crown
It is easy for you to breathe
You are a miracle
You are powerful
You get to say when
And that time is not now
Praise God, hallelu
Nights like these give me hope
Bring me visions of her leaving
Walking out of Kaiser, never to look back again
We take her to quality care
Treat the cancer outpatient
Beat it back until we've hit every item on the bucket list
Tahiti and Miss Emily's in the Bahamas
Red carpets and Emmys
She went out there and is directing these shows
We are a family
Playing bid whist until the wee hours of the morning
Remembering a morning we almost lost her
But didn't.
She is here.
She is here.
Praise God.
She is a miracle.

Healing Hands
for my Mother

My mother is a healer
Her hands adorned with life lines
Read along honey palms
She knows how to heal
How to transform my pain to power
My mother is a miracle worker.

The new year's morning I could have sworn
Death had come for me,
Skeleton fingers cold and outstretched
Chattering teeth and sweaty brow

She laid her hands
On my temple
And solved what Western medicine could not—
My mother knows the power of unconditional love.

Forever with the right words
Her hands stew and cook and stir
So much care into me.
Her world-famous mac 'n' cheese and collard greens
Feed my body and spirit.
She tells me to have faith—
I have all I need and more.
She reminds me I am loved,
Often.
Sometimes,
That is all the healing
I need.
My mother is supportive
Her hands hold me up
On even my most broken days.
She gives.
Selflessly.
Says she learned that recipe

From my grandmother
What an honor to descend
From such a line of women.
I am my mother's daughter
My hands look like hers.
Of all the people in the Universe
How lucky I am that she chose me.

Tfairyfly

When my cousin Tanea passed away
My grieving aunt gave me many of her belongings:
The rainbow Snoopy piggy bank without a stopper
The newspaper clipping with her smiling portrait
The red and blue Adidas jacket Grandpa used to wear
Tanea looked so fly in it
The older I get the more the memories fade
But the love always remains.

Auntie Fundisha gave me Tanea's dream catcher
A red and feathered, beaded ornament
First hung because it looked pretty
Now pays homage to my favorite cousin
Makes her seem not as gone
Not so far away.

We hung it in our old apartment
And oh, what dreams.

My fiancé and I took it down
After the nightmares got too heavy
After I saw a circle of ancestors
Surround my uncle a week before his passing

After the ghosts haunted our dreams
With their terrifying stories
And incomplete pasts.

We moved.
Here, now, in our new apartment around the corner
We hung Tanea's dream catcher
Just above our bed, on a hook that seemed perfectly placed
And the dreams came.

Along with the ghosts and cobwebbed buildings
The dusty lights and older people I did not recognize
Offering pecan pies and carrot cakes
They tell me stories in my sleep.
I try to stay present with them
To listen
Knowing there are whispers of stories I missed
When they were here, alive.
Now all I have are these visions
Rooting up who I am
Searching for some glimpse of family,
Flashlights probing the corners of my dark, dim mind
for answers.

Grief, Nostalgia, Joy

"Mr. Jones and Me" comes on the radio
And I think of my ancestors
My cousin Tanea, Grandma, Grandpa, Uncle Bobby.
I remember what loss hurts like
I am familiar with the way grief
Comes and goes in tides
How he spies you
Basking in the sunlight of your perfectly pleasant day
And crumples your face like a piece of paper
He squeezes your heart, wrung out and soggy
Wet with tears that find fresh new ways to well
Even so many years later.
Nostalgia is an old friend
She touches brief smiles on your lips
Reminds you of the wonder you once enjoyed
Running along the gate to her door
Hand to hand, foot to ground
Flying over her heels and laughing.
Joy takes you by the hand
Boisterous and loud
She welcomes you with open arms and a laughter flush with delight
Says forget your sorrow
Says this ache
This pain is but a temporary symptom
She reminds me there is still beauty
Joy guides me to revel in this moment
This moment. This here. This now.
She fills my cup with warmth and sunshine
Acknowledging the sheer hope of our existence.
Chirping birds and radiant color
She reminds me to have total gratitude
Each memory a reminder
We've only got today.

For Mick on Her Anniversaire

You were a light
A force on this planet
Touching the lives of all around you
You made me feel at home
In foreign places
Our voices learned in other languages
Met at the crossroads of communication.
Between my broken phrases
Voulez vous voir une photo?
And your school-day British English
Happy birthday, Yazmin. With love of your Mick
We met somewhere in the middle
Spoke Spanish, broke barriers
Your presence is sorely missed today.
With so much love to give
It's a wonder your heart
Had all that extra room
To teach me how to make soufflés and sole meunière
I am a better person because I met you
Thank you for the laughter
And your infectious fighter spirit.
I have never met anyone more determined to give
You taught me what it means to live
To fight for a life worth living
Tu es une force
Une brillance / lumière en la nuit
I try to write in French, but I'm not sure it translates
I wonder if you understand me.
Since I'm sure you've already made best friends with everyone up there
Please give *une gros bisous a mon grand-mère aussi et*
Tell me. Does God have Rosetta Stone?
One day I'll be able to *écrit cette poème en juste français et*
Regarde! Mon français est mieux! (kinda.)
Merci beaucoup Mick pour tous
You brought love into my life
Literally and figuratively

Mon vie est mieux grâce à toi.
Je t'aime.

Dear Straight People

after Denice Frohman

Congratulations.

You made it to this century without having this conversation. How
you made it here with these antiquated beliefs is beyond me, but
for some clarification and general goodwill toward building bridges
between us, I have a few questions to get that dialogue started. . . .

1.

Why are you so afraid of sexuality? We're not mythological beings
who'll infect you with our queerness like some bubonic plague. Some
of us are queer. Get over it.*

        *since something tells me it's not actually that easy. . . .

2.

Why are you so obsessed with seeing images of yourself in the me-
dia? And why do the queer characters always have to die? (Further-
more, why do the Black ones always die first?!)*

        *follow up to the follow up, why aren't there any queer
        people of color in media controlled by you? Why are you so
        intent on erasing our history?

3.

Why do you always ask when I knew? Did you ever have to come out
as straight? For the last time, I'm bisexual. Why do I have to come
out with each new partner?

4.

Why do you glare so hard when I hold my partner's hand in public,
no less when I kiss her? Do I stare at you while you sloppily tongue
down gal pal number 682? How does it feel to canoodle in public?
Y'all look so cozy. What's it like to kiss your significant other without
fear of bodily harm or harassment? Must be nice.

5.

Nah, you ain't invited! What makes you think you have an all-access pass to my bedroom? This isn't E! Entertainment, Bravo. We are not here for your enjoyment. Hard pass on that threesome with you and your girlfriend.

6.

Why do you think you can "convert" me? Just because I'm bi does not mean I'm into everyone, especially not you, boo.

7.

Why do you confuse gender and sexuality so often? They are not one and the same. Stop asking "who's the guy?" I know you can't imagine relationships outside the fragility of your heteronormative "lifestyle" (ooh, that word stings, doesn't it?). It just doesn't work like that.

8.

Why do you only back off when I say I have a boyfriend? Do I have to be "owned" by another man for you to get that I'm just not that into you?

9.

Why do you keep telling me I'm finally straight now that I have a male partner? My bisexuality doesn't disappear when I commit to one person.

10.

Why is marriage such a big deal to you? Is monogamy the only narrative you understand? (Your 50 percent divorce rate might say otherwise— all tea, all shade). Do you really think the only thing we care about is marriage? That piece of paper doesn't change anything for the countless queer youths living on Skid Row, the Black and brown trans bodies floating up in rivers of blood around this nation, the many cases of workplace discrimination and the immeasurable health disparities that plague our people. A wedding does not solve that.

11.

Why do you think your religion is an excuse to dictate my life? Get out of my face, you Christmas-and-Easter-only "Christian." My God is a queer Black feminist Spirit, and She is a reflection of me. Step up your self-love.

12.

Furthermore, why is it so hard for you to understand intersectionality? We can be more than one thing at one time. I am a Black, bisexual woman, poet, activist, warrior, goddess; I contain multitudes.

13.

Do I look like a professor? I know that every argument can be a "teachable moment," but sometimes I just want to check my socials and have a kiki without having to break down critical race and gender theory. Please. Read a book.

14.

Dear straight people, stop asking me to choose. No I am not greedy, no I am not confused, no I am not a cheater—I am bisexual. I love without limits.

15.

Dear my people, stop asking me to choose. No I am not greedy, I am not confused, no I am not a cheater—I am bisexual. I love beyond binaries.

16.

Dear queer white people, Black lives matter. Some of us are Black too. Some of us are queer too.

Dear allies, this poem ain't for you. But come and get your friend.

We Stand

a Pride Commission

We stand on the shoulders of those
Radical warriors whose unwavering vision
For a world where we are free to love
Became more important than the hurl of slurs
That bigotry bashed over our heads like bricks.
Don't you remember Stonewall?

We have lost so many in the battle against AIDS,
hate crimes, violence, addiction, homelessness,
sexual assault, and suicide

They say if you don't know where you come from
You can't know where you are going

We are here because they were here

Don't you forget our history
We are a people who were built to survive
We thrive, loving without limits
Descendants from a long line of soldiers

Strong enough to fight

They marched and they rallied
Chanting for a change
Staging sit-ins, signing petitions
Taking back the night

We stood together
From Christopher Street, east to west
We made a real home for ourselves
From rainbow flag to Pride parade

Our community is built of so much more
Than just the LGBT
We are rainbow enough to include
Every shade of color
Embrace our difference
Regardless of how we love
Or gender-bend
With allies walking hand in hand

We are family
We are here
We exist

The future belongs to us
What will our legacy be?

Forgiveness

You are a war
I barely survived
And even still
Especially still
I forgive you
And free myself.

Word to These Words

I breed art like my soul depends on it,
clawing every ounce of what I've got from
this belly of diamonds and half-empty matter,
I am birthing strange realities,
a blur of self-made alchemy,
conjured only in REM nightmares, warnings of dreams so soaked in vision
they are cradled heavy in bloody-palmed umbili-
called wet poeming.

when I dream in art,
I am connected places

other than self,
other than world,
when I let myself whirl
in this storm of wombed metaphor.
these words reveal raveling,
a brutal cloud reveling,
of rivers of unborn longing
billowing infant under my skirt.
with curly hair, bright eyes, and
sun-rose in white lies,
these poems flower haunting,
an homage to yellow wallpaper
splintering in the light of an honest dew.

these words are the pews
where I lay my heart wholly,
a delivered communion of unborn fantasia
spilling and marching like cotton from uterus,
birthed against all that is reason.
on window panes shattered,
collapsed in what matters,
these words
are a damning hope Spring(ing);
a relished salvation,

delicious temptation,
this poem is a misconstrued darkness.

but write past the silence,
alluringly frightening so brightly,
my cortex stretches bold and strengthens,
forming worlds inflused with cosmos
flexing power in the knowing
that this art is homemade therapy.
so in the name of Love and poetry,
these words dare to hold my throat hostage,
stringing knives about my collarbone,
begging to bleed themselves out of me.

Wakiesha's Poem

On the one-year anniversary
Of yet another Black death
A Black woman is risen

In the voice of her people
She walks in our steps
And lives in our movement
We say her name
Wakiesha Wilson
We say her name
Demanding justice now
Knowing Black death and cover-ups
Sound the same across this country
We lift her up and make her visible

On the day of yet another Black death behind bars

On the day that yet another Black woman's murder is deemed suicide

On the day the LAPD rules themselves in conduct

We grieve and cry
and then dream
(Because sometimes the dreaming gives us clarity
of visions to work toward in the waking)

And in my dreams
I pray an alternate universe exists
And somewhere
In this timeline
A telephone rings
And a mother picks up
And passes the phone to her grandson
Who says *come on home, Mama*
And she does

And she wishes her beloved aunt the happiest of birthdays
And she lives
In this timeline
A mother does not sit by a phone
And show up to court
Looking for a daughter
That the police would never allow to return
Lord, let there be a Universe

Without the cover up, without the abuse, the murder
Before the red, white, and blue lights signal
the end of another Black life

Lord, please let there be another timeline
Where the police who killed Wakiesha
Are held accountable
Where the LAPD no longer terrorize our community

God damn. Please let there be an alternate universe
And in it a timeline
Where a mother receives a phone call
And that phone call leads to a court date
And that court date leads to a fair process
And a mother drives her daughter back
And she goes home

And on this Resurrection Sunday
Somewhere a phone rings
A mother goes home to her son
And Black joy is synonymous with a reimagined justice

And instead of prison bars and over policed states
The community is supported and healed and whole
And on this Resurrection Sunday

We celebrate a life that got to live to her fullest capacity
And on this timeline
the ancestors smile and say, *well done*

We'll see you in a good long while
But take your time, baby.
And we do.

For Black Girls Who Have Lost Their Ribbons

after Toni Morrison
for Dasani

This is for little Black girls who have lost their ribbons.
For whom grief is an ever-present houseguest
Strolling in with the breeze
Who have known that the price of our freedom
Has always been soaked in a red sacrifice
Who have seen face to face the other end of shotgun barrels
Even while opening mouths for help at neighborhood doorways
Watching
On this soil
That they lied to us and falsely named home.
This is for little Black girls
Who are worlds away
In a shared studio apartment
With a family of eight
Tending their mothers' children
Barely finding a way to stay awake and out of trouble
In troubled school hallways.
This is for Black girls
Who go to corner stores on their way home from school
Just wanting to buy sour candy and soda
And exit this world on the back of bodega floors.
This is for Black girls at college parties
Who are taken by entire teams of boys with no repercussions
For Black girls fighting for "our" freedom in Iraq
And coming back bruised in body bags and cover-up stories.
No one investigates our trauma.
For these little Black girls
There is no trust in the word *safety*
No rest from the constant glance over shoulder
No trusting the smiles of white men
In white houses who offer false promises
Knowing that the way they vote
The way they live
The way they take

Are traditions that are steeped in the red, white, and blue of colonialist imperialism
Our hands, always the ones to reach out to the other side, singed by the fires of all their "good" intentions.
This is for little Black girls
With curls in matted hair
And ribbons lost in the breeze
Or found at the surface of bottomless rivers
Godless that they now be
They are lost in a system that does not care for poor people
Black people
Brown people
Queer people
Trans people
Our people are dying and my heart
Full as a gallon tank
Spills in flames along the highway
All over the street, on the floor, in my bedroom, on my pillow
Reading stories of little Black girl ghosts
And all I can think is
It is not enough to cry
It is not enough to cry
I don't have any answers
Just an angry sort of scream
A history of curdled blood and magic
Born with a belly full of fed up
Screaming *how are we not moved enough to move?*
If not for our daughters with lost ribbons from their hair
Our little Black girls, then whom?
I wonder what it will take
What will happen
When we are all
Bold enough to rage.

Challenger

Something deep down in my soul said, "Cry, girl"
—Etta James

Today was a typical day at Challenger
We read our students Dr. Seuss
Based our poetry workshop on a childhood classic
(Knowing not many of our boys even had one)
Laughed when they said Seuss had bars
While behind bars
We try to give our students poems
The gift of their own story
In their own words
And today
Miracle that it was
Almost everyone wrote a poem or rap or story
Oh, the places they'd been
Oh, the places they'd hope to go
When they grow up . . . *if*, they said.
What wonderful dreams they'd imagined.
We had what we would call
A perfect day.

And then as we were just about to head back home
Ms. Peterson pulled us to the side
To ask if we had heard about . . .
And right there
In the middle of our clear and perfect day
The sadness snatched the air from our throats
No idea what to say or do
We hear the story of yet another life stolen
And our world stops
The air crowding in all around us.
And somehow the haughty earth
Has the audacity to keep spinning

And you just want everyone to stop and witness
The tragedy of a young life spilling red around us
We were just, we were just sittin' there
Teaching him poems
And helping him tell his story—
The stanza cut short, without an end.

I was just, I was just
I was just writing
I know I am grateful for the symphonies
My students compose every Tuesday
How lucky I am to bear witness

But what good is a poem
When our students no longer have the breath
To speak their truth

I'd rather be blind
Than see one more of my students go down that road to the cell
To a state-sanctioned grave.

We were just driving to Baskin-Robbins for our lunch break
And I saw a dead crow's wings flapping in the wind
And I should have known.
We played the students Etta James as our workshop wrapped up.
Something told me it was over
And it was.

Curling Rage

You're mad at the world,
I know.
You can do bad all by yourself
You want to hang on to that anger
Rage is an easy outlet
Your body a hurricane of daggers
A tornado of fear
Violence
Curling thunder in your knuckles.
I know
Closed fists seem to make more sense
When you disappear the humanity from their faces
As opposed to the hard work it takes to
Calm that rumble growling in your belly.
It's difficult to truly build community,
I know.
But before you spring scorpion
With all that pent-up, misplaced energy,
Wipe the red from your eyes
Sing a lullaby to the bite bated in your breath
Say goodnight
Breathe for a moment.
Clear out all that white noise
Make your way back to your center.
You just might find
That inner piece
That inner voice
That knows peace.

An Ode to Octavia
(Or On Dreaming New Religions or One Way
I Learned God Could Have M(any) Names)

. . . the Destiny of Earthseed
is to take root among the stars.
—*Octavia E. Butler,* Parable of the Sower

I am told I am reading science fiction
As if it is impossible to imagine
A Black woman
Seated amongst the stars
A blooming bright seed
Sewn into the history of
This darkened tapestry of sky
Shining in the ether of a new and crafted reality
Who knew that God could have my name?
A dream by any other name is still called,
I am called—to action
To love. To trust in
Myself. Finally!
Told I got some kinda nerve
Tone it down
How dare I shine?
How dare I dream, grow, change?
Sayin' who am I to rise up?
How dare I fall on that good ground
Springing up to thrive?

Unsettle Your Bones

Enter no-man's-land
Shed your technology
Lose track of time
Watch the sun rise
From the tail end of
A sky chock-full of
Cookies-and-cream stars
Forget yourself
Pack a bag for the unknown
For once in your life
Get out of your comfort zone
The world is waiting
Just there
On the other side
For the love of God
Escape
Go
Travel
Unsettle your bones.

III

Filling

Afrika Burn

It's raining fire
And still Pompeii plays the classics
The lighthouse shines the way
To a good time
As Amsterdam plays '70s soul
Bubbles and Bass wakes us all
With a little sun-risen bubbly
Welcoming with open arms
We all gather beneath
The burning man
Holding hands
With heads gaped skywards
Our mouths an open-marveled wonder
Our hearts
Split wide open and full
Love exists in the spark
Of air between us all.
We are
One.
This is our Gift
This connection
This moment
Burn Magic
Under a glowing sky
"Dream the light and sleep tight"
I hold you close
And remember always
We take a piece of each other
Everywhere we go
Loving
And keeping that love
Safe inside
In awe, in delight
Remembering the moments
We've shared with each other
Having spent this moment in our lives

Together
Together
Together
We are
Here
Because of each other
Thank you
Thank you
Thank you
I am here
Because you are here
Love to you
Love to you
Love to you
To this soil
To Higher Power
To that which crossed our paths and
Brought us each to the other
Love to you love to you
This is all we have
All we have is worth giving
Praise be for
Love love love
How grateful I am for you.
My soul sleeps well
With the burning memory of our connection.

Let's Go Dutch

1. *Ik ben mezelf niet*
(translation)
"I am not myself"
Image is everything
And I present to you
The whole
Part of me
That wants to be perfect.
Warning
I am more flaw than perfection
More human than idol
I am still on a journey to my center.

2. *Ik moet mijzelf*
"I will enjoy myself"
I realize I am flawed
That I can expect no more from you
Than I can from myself
If I don't protect my best interests
Who will?
Today I will be selfish
I will eat all the cheese on the platter
I will have two more glasses of wine
And will please myself
First. And finally
I will not apologize.

3. *Wie ben jij?*
"Who are you?"
Take off your mask
I want to get to know you
Let's *take off our cool* together
Let's make our truer selves
Uncomfortable
In a different language
Our inhibitions are merely
Road maps to our deepest desires.

Communication

I like to dabble in tongues
Savor the way a new word sounds in my mouth
Swilling it around from side to side
I appreciate the uncomfortable way
A new phrase will sometimes trip, fall
Wobble in my head
And finally stumble in exclamations
Communicate with me!
I understand!
Let's share stories together.
I love to comprehend a new language
Different than my own
I am delighted at the way new words sound
When they fight their way dogged from my lips
Clumsy and loud
(More than likely wrong)
There are certain sounds my American tongue
Is not yet equipped to form
But I am willing to learn.
Teach me your language
And we will sing songs of magic and understanding.

A Sacred Prayer Made Manifest

Fingers lingering over keyboards
Yearning to touch your body
Instead, none of these words will satiate
The bloodlust, the desire brought forth, the absolute hunger
Craving more and more
Your fingertips dance along my shoulder blades
And I unravel
Fingers flit like knitted yarn
And I am fully entangled
Wrapped up in your snare
Oh so deliciously
Tied up
Your fingertips tease every part of me
Tiny little fires alight
Across my body
You drape your arms around me
Like this is where I belong
Like I could really fall
Like this could be the destination
Like what does the world even know about energy
thisdeepthisfullthislightning
The world ablaze around us
You pull me in, put me out
Quench this thirst
In your water I am clean
Made whole, our union a holy sacrament
A sacred prayer made manifest

Remembrance

My lips on her spine
Her cheeks resting on my upper thighs
Bodies curled into each other
I write it down so I remember
So that when we part
Perhaps instead of careening off the cliff
Of *this could never work*
And *I miss you*
I can come back to this memory
Of this soft and lovely morning
Our bodies breathing in unison
Rising and falling
Deeper and deeper in love

Once Haunted

Dear ghosts,
How small you look
From this side of once haunted.

Life is grand
See how I soar now?
You don't scare me anymore.

Frost and Bone

First, the sweater
To show you I am not a woman of frost and bone
But of muscle and skin, heart and ardor.

I am real.

Then, the skirt
A pull of string
Cotton billowing
Loosened around my ankles
I stopped running kilometers ago
Next, the shirt strap
Toyed beneath index finger and thumb
Hands pulling fabric from torso
To the feathered skirt on the floor
I am a halo enshrined to only you
Nothing else remains
And now I am bare before you
Naked and honest as your fingers laced in mine
Eyes locked in passion and trust
I will not hide from you
Only love lives here.

The Answer
for David

Your name tumbles from my mouth
Like the smile I once thought was too clumsy
To fall into anything less than tragic:
Magic, ocean, home
These are the words I conjure when I think of you.
Collapsed in a sea of smiles
Your name is the discovery on the other side of broken;
Breaking is only one of temporary bruises
I've had many
But most importantly, you:

Are water in a desert
The swarm of butterflies leaping from my throat
The moment my eyes open
Lingering on your lashes
And yours open.
Open
Me? (ha!)
Like a book
Or like trust
That last bastion of pride any of us have left
Mere offerings at your altar
I lay me at your feet
(and don't even have to warn, *tread carefully*)
You must have known this poem was coming
This moment when I would pour out all my secrets
Oil and incense supplicating from my mouth
The smoke of your name crawling toward the air like a prayer
Or the answer
I have learned
Happiness is a day of nothing with you
A lifetime of everything worth anything
Love
Love
Love!

This is what it sounds like when I shout your name across the valley
What it feels like when I finally call your name
And you answer.

Love to the Powerhouse Black Women of Black Lives Matter

Those who put their bodies on the front lines of justice every single day
Deep love to all the organizers facing hateful attacks from all sides:
the state, white supremacists, and all their witting accomplices
Even when the world is intent on tearing us down
Even when it be our own (internalized misogynoir is a helluva drug)
Shout out to those who do the work anyway
Who show up every Tuesday, every Wednesday, every Thursday,
every Saturday, every week, all these years
Demanding police accountability in rooms they insist on shutting us
out of
When folks roll their eyes and allow yet another killer cop off the hook
Love for the countless hours of unpaid labor
To those Black women who mourn and then organize
Who know that our collective efforts are a sacred call and duty
Love to those who ousted the most murderous police chief in the
nation (yeah, Chief Moore, you next) and pushed out the most callous
district attorney who refused to prosecute those who would steal the
lives of over six hundred of our loved ones here in LA
Love to the ones who work to end police associations and hold the
flame to profit-centered politicians
Bought by these fake-ass "unions"
Love to those who sharpened the blade
That cut $150 million from the police budget and made them reckon
with a people's budget
Love to those who publicly called for sheriff–civilian oversight
The ones who demand accountability in real, tangible ways that
impact our people
Love to those who planted bunk beds in the street and grew the push
to halt the $2 billion jail expansion project
The dandelion seeds of which blew and grew to Ballot Measure R
Forcing LA County to invest in alternatives to incarceration and
granting power for investigating sheriff misconduct
Love to those who organize and empower the formerly incarcerated
and system-impacted families

Who got thousands released from jail cells at the start of coronavirus
The angel architects who crafted Measure J
Snatching 10 percent of the county budget away from killer cops
And forced this city to invest in mental health, jobs, substance abuse
support, youth development, and more
Shout out to the mothers, the mothers, the mothers, and grand-
mothers and siblings and aunties and cousins and partners who said
not my baby, not one more, I just don't want no more folks to die
Love to the Black teens in the Youth Vanguard who said *no more cops
in our schools*
Love to the activists who ended random searches in LAUSD
Whose vision for our children included counselors and nurses and
who demanded we end the school-to-prison pipeline and defund
those who would steal the lives of our children
Love to the Black women who shift public policy in this nation
From local decertification bills and nationwide acts to divest from
policing and invest in our community
Love to those who help us breathe (what an act)
Who help us dream
Who show us our magnificence on silver screens
And *New York Times* bestsellers lists
When They Call You a Terrorist
Love to the Black women who teach
Who lead us to liberation
Love to the women of Black Lives Matter
Who bring their whole hearts to this thankless movement
Who burn the midnight oil every single day
Who unravel white supremacy thread by tangled thread
And weave a tapestry of hope and real change across this nation.
Don't get distracted. Don't be disheartened.
When the world is intent on bringing you down,
Be encouraged. We are winning. And they shook.
Be encouraged.
I see and lift you up, sis
Value your contribution to this planet, to our people
Love always to the abolitionists
Who usher our way to freedom.

Beloved

Rather than give her daughter to that life,
she killed it. If in her deep maternal love
she felt the impulse to send her child
back to God, to save it from coming woe,
who shall say she had no right not to do so?
—Lucy Stone on behalf of Margaret Garner

Old narratives tell the story
Of mothers who would rather kill their children
Than subject them to a life of slavery
Whose love waded in waters so deep
They could not return

This, then, is for the mothers
Who survive ghost-almosts
Swimming behind closed lids
Seeing invisible futures

Seeing their daughters' futures
Entire lines of families
Hanging from invisible trees

She lives, though.
Swims behind
Closed eyelids
Corrects "kids"
Mistakes
Dreams
For reality
Reads
Beloved Toni
Triggers on
Trains
Bound for
Southern
Waters.
Feels

All that history
Swimming up
Around her
Faces
Bloody
Rivers
Wading
Children
Troubled
Waters
Visions
Afloat
Alive
Laughing
Dancing
(At long last)
Some
How?
Better
Bitter
Now awake
She be memory
Faded letters
Bottled up and
Shipwrecked
Floating out
To a merciful sea.

A Prayer for Our Someday Children

You, descendant of Haitian revolution and survivor of southern shackles
You, who have the prayers of freedom fighters and joy lovers encamped
about you
Abolition baptized in your bloodstream
You—yes, you, my love—are the most tender miracle.
A sunshine rainbow gathering glitter in the growing
Our queer Black family an unapologetic continuation of all that has
come before,
By bloodline and by choice
In spite of what we may not have received
From those who did not have the capacity to live so freely
Because of ancestors who gave love in such abundance
You, my dear, my most sweet and nurtured dream
The hope and healing of tomorrow and today.

Please remember always
You matter, my love.
As your parents, we model what loving out loud looks like so you will
never have to fear the judgment of your own shadow
Nor hide from the deepest and truest parts of your heart that yearn to
love without boundary
We choose to break chains and live openly, honestly,
and free of inhibition
We define what family means
And craft our own space for liberation
So that you will not be afraid
To express your truest self in all your glory
Nor dim your light for some convenience
There is no room for shame here
Only questions that eventually yield answers
Only love that holds us tight
And demands a call for justice as our given right.

I pray you know a world without police violence, racism, homophobia,
misogyny, transphobia
The kind of hate that attempts to stamp out our people

This is why we fight.
This is why we give with all our might to ensure this place be safe
harbor for you when you arrive

And try as we may to protect you
To hold you in our arms and on our backs
I know the world is waiting for you with a brick
Beloved. Brilliant that you are,
Some will attempt to cage your sun and call it night
Do not believe the lies
My dear, *mon cœur,* the very piece of me that lives and thrives and
breathes and beams
Knows that when they try us, and they will,
Remember this prayer and affirmation:

Our love is stronger than fear
Our love sets us free.

Breaking in Silence
for Simone

Confession: I see a therapist.
Every Monday afternoon
At 12 p.m. on the dot
I find myself on a green couch
In Studio City, spilling my guts to a woman named Rande.
I've been seeing her since June, since Uncle Bobby passed, since the abortion,
Since life decided to get so damned hard.
It helps.

Part of removing the fear
Is confronting it out loud
Name the trauma in all its forms
Shout its name in the mirror
Candy Man

Why is our self-care so taboo?

Mental health care in the Black community
Is so rarely discussed. So rarely confronted
Why are the people who judge us the most
(re: homophobic pastors)
The ones we're told to talk to when shit goes down?
Mind, body, and spirit are important, yes, but

Professional medical advice
Is seen as a white people problem
Black women shoulder the burden of our struggle like Atlas
Mule of the world
Our cheerful exteriors
Shaded by the deep shadows of our pain
Did you know even the strongest among us can crack?
I'm done breaking in silence.

We save so
many others
And forget to
Save ourselves.

Should We Ever Forget

Everything around us contains material that was once made up of a star. The cells in our bodies, the air we breathe, and materials that make up the planets in our solar system are all linked to the stars through chemical elements.
—*Griffith Observatory*

Should we ever forget we are not alone
All we ever need do is look to the stars
The sun, the moon
All reminders of how we are connected
Tiny astrological points in the sky.
What makes me human
Is the same chemical arrangement
That makes you so.
We are but specks of stardust
Twinkling in the skyline
Of a brilliant Earth
So many light-years away.
Our light,
A burning ball of bright life, destined to dissipate
Before the blink of an eye
On the brink of time, running down a glass corridor
Like the sand of an hourglass
At some hour
We will extinguish.
Our bones melted down
To speckled dust
Our spirits
Exploring the wide-open ether
Of an alternate reality, the afterlife
We are comprised of so many potential miracles
A spark this world will only experience
This once in a lifetime.
Be sure to make the most of it.
Remember that even though you may feel lonely
You are not alone.
So wherever you are tonight
From NYC to Paris

From London to DC
From Philly to Séte
From the Bay to LA
Look up at the sky
From so far away it all looks the same.
Share this moment with me.
Know that I am here too
Thinking of you.

Quarantine

These days find me writing
Procrastinating on writing
Catchin' up on my stories
I sleep to my heart's content
At long last I turn inward
Tend to my own garden
Water myself first
Nourish my body with good food and care
I treat me real good, baby
And oh, what an indulgence
I take myself out to only the finest places
The kitchen, the couch, the bed
I spend quality time with me
Excavate the wounds
Generational pain exposed
I am healing, understand my history
Accept and mourn. Find peace.
Speak to my family daily
Love on my community often
There is nothing out there
That I did not already have in me.
I engage whole revolutions from my balcony
Per Angela, "Do my work where I am"
Show I care by staying in
Here I find all the answers
Ask about me
The question leads to more
Abundance flows freely
See how all I had to do was stay still
And listen?

My Spirit is awake
My soul is at rest
Selah.
Oh, this feels so damn good.

Awkward

My feet never know how to move on the dance floor
Shuffling from side to side
Awkward
They lead me to crash-landings
On the moon
Walking backwards
Someone asked me to
"Turn up"
The volume? I asked
I grew up around a lot of white people
Have been constantly ridiculed
For not being Black enough.
Have always wondered
For whom?
I live in the in-between
Slurs like "Oreo"
Have followed me
From grade school to present
Though I cannot even fathom
What people could possibly have against
Really delicious cookies
Or being grammatically correct.
I do not fit into one neat little box
Do not know how to separate and divide
The aspects of self that make me whole.
I am still amazed that despite the odds
Somehow, by an impossible act of God
And the stubborn, rugged skin of my teeth
I have managed to unpack
And settle into this body I call home.

I, Too
after Langston Hughes

I, too, belong
I, too, preach pulpit prophet
Great gold organs before me
And the souls of Black folk behind me
I, too,
Speak rivers
Holy water pouring from my mouth
I, too, am holy
Healthy, whole, and holy
Worthy
Of sharing story
Queering spaces
A communion of community
With every shade of rainbow
Creed and color
I, too, listen
Channel God
Channel Spirit
I, too, am Spirit
Am all the change I was looking for
I, too, am healer
Make whole the pain
Bear witness
Inspire
I, too, am path-paving
Ground-shaking
Language-reframing
I, too, self-love
Transform
Create in me my own image
I, too, am history
Brave enough to speak
Been called to preach
Freely
Poetry is a gospel

I, too, be saving lives
Bringing heart
Can I get an Amen?
Can I get a soul clap?
I, too, am gift
Embrace my calling
I, too, am called
I church
I praise
I, too, be Black tradition
Nontraditional
I be grateful
I, too, am valid
And here
At the shores of my mother's garden
Ocean rushing rapid through my spirit
I come to know Universe
Indeed
I see that I, too, am God.

The Stardust and the Scatter
after Valerie June

Man on elevator
Say he see my light
I say that's just his
Reflecting mine
We all just out here, mirrors
Searching to be seen
Understood
Underneath
All this sadness
There too's been hella joy
There too's been plenty dark
Places I don't show you
When I'm skating in the park
These eyes have watered
Rivers, traveled seas
Just to see
What bliss life has to offer
A different point of view
Perspective provides possibility
How do we all get free?
Lawd knows I'm not perfect
Grace, grace, mercy, please
I'm still healing too
Do the best with what I got
Poetry and passion
Peals of laughter
Play on purpose
Brief and tender
Moments of reprieve
I don't know how much time
I got left here, but in the interim
Find me dancing
All off-beat and merry
I'm just feeling my way through
One moment at a time

The stardust and the scatter
Love in such abundance

Vignette

1.

I lean into her body like I belong
Her lips already a distant memory on my cheek
We are both bathed in pink
All cotton candy smiles
Moonlit and full of promises sweet as new beginnings
Prince sighs "If I Was Your Girlfriend"
And we sing roses around his favorite rink
We are in the middle of a break
Catching our breath before we
Glide circles around conventional norms
I am out of breath, incredulous
This is a life I get to live.
Unapologetic, free. Polyamory is a new jumpsuit
And y'all, this is my style.

2.

She smiles as if she knows it is goodbye
Knows she wants more and has yet to tell me
Like she doesn't know a heart can expand
Like she doesn't know a heart can be a home too
Like she doesn't know I can build whole new rooms
As if she doesn't know I have already built the new walls
Torn down the structure
Refurbished, revamped. Made room, built a whole new wing
Taken flight and soared
I have fallen, and here in the sunlight
Our curls dripping sea-foam and joy
This sun-smiling photo
Beyoncé and Jay-Z sing *let's make love in the summertime*
And how glorious that last sun
An unnamed seedling, still growing but gone
Bathed in potential and meaning
A love we almost had, or did.
Even if only for a wisp of a moment

3.

I take a solo selfie in all white
After all, I am a wife already
My curls are perfectly moisturized, this cotton hugs my hips
This gold glints glitter on my neck
On my mama, on my hood, I look fly, I look good
Zora's words echo: *How could she deny [herself] the pleasure of my company?*
And how many days I took that personally
Held that rejection so deep,
I almost made it mine
Lord knows how long it took me to get to this space of self-love and
acceptance.
How sure I am of my own power, my needs.
I am singing Eryn Allen Kane
Have mercy, have mercy
I am clear, poly, and sure.
Full of love that flows from the inside
I am a well, and like water I go
Deeper and deeper into myself.

Grateful

I love the way my pen finds paper early in the morning
For family, a loving, supporting den of lion women
I am grateful for my single-mother upbringing
Black women, queer women of color
Other mothers who raised me as their own
Lifted me from clueless chick to soulful soldier warrior
They taught me how to fight,
How to love.
Man, I love Love.
The way it settles on his smile when he genuinely laughs.
The way her hand feels like a revolution every time it is in mine.
I love laughter,
Wide-mouthed and full.
The way it fills in my belly like a pastry pie
J'aime la nourriture:
French croissants, *chèvre aux raisins*
How lucky I am to have tasted the finest from other regions.
Oh, how I love this planet,
Love the way she drapes compassion
Around these Cali beach–browned shoulders
Like a faux fur jacket
Did I mention I love my fro?
Unwieldy and wild
My hair don't belong to nobody but me.
I am so pleased with the woman I am becoming
Grateful for a space of my own
With a future as bright as flame
Like the sun on my NoHo porch chair during morning meditations.
I am grateful for the ocean
In her sea-salted waves I first found home.

I found a home in my own body
I am grateful I am Black and queer and woman.
Glad I have a voice
Glad I fought to express it
Grateful for the journey

And for those who've joined in with me
Kin who share with me a network of love and song
All across this planet.
I am grateful for poetry
Who let me cry into her shoulder
Pages absorbing every ink splotch of my pain.
I am thankful for the ancestors
For the love they endured to make sure I am here
I am here, y'all.
Naked and honest
Bare as my feet standing tree trunk on this soil
Thank God, whoever She may be—
For Audre, for Alice, for bell and Staceyann
Thank Spirit for sending other women warriors
Who gave voice to my experience
And taught me to do the same.
What a privilege to be an artist
A door-to-door salesman
Knocking with heart on sleeve
I am grateful to be an instrument
Open and receptive to the muse.
I am grateful
I am grateful
I am full.

IV

Floating

Upon Waking from a Nap Underwater

In this water. I emerge alive
Baptized. Once spoke in holy(?)
Tongues, now speak different
Language. Still. Wholly divine

Entwined in my lovers' mouths
And limbs. Whispering wet truths
Spoken across the gender divide

God knows my heart. My desire(s)
Plural. Speaking truths of wanton lust
Deliberate and afraid of nothing

Pastor Swancy lied. Told me I would die
But (Audre) Lorde told me different
See how I embrace my difference
Look at my float now. Breathing underwater.
Gloating bi, see how my lover's limbs hold me
God whispering in the air-locked space
Between us. And is this not
(what) God
Intended. For Her creation to create
New ways to admit
We are here and alive

And should that not be a celebration?

Our bodies, caught.
Knees knockin', spines spinnin', souls arching,
Aching around each other
Caught up in a Ghost
A holy spell, a forgotten southern magic

Ain't no massa's religion
Some spirit we were forced to conjure
On some white man's plantation

In some white man's "native" tongue
his god (all lowercase) all white

Did we forget the visions B(l)ack
In our dreams?
I relearn my power.
This love, a reflection rippling
In waves of ancient waters.
History now present. I am present

And whole and clean and here
My body a vessel born to float.

Freedom

How do I live free in this Black body?
—Ta-Nehisi Coates

What would freedom taste like?
Look like? How does it sound
When I walk along the shores
Of a reclaimed sea
Does my body,
Browned and painted like the night,
Remember its sacrifice?

How does it unlearn the terror
Beaten into our bloodline?

How do we heal?
How do we recover our bodies
And claim them as our own?

What is it to own my own body?
To feel my lungs swell with daring air
To speak and act like I was the standard,
Like I was born safe,
Like the world was meant for me,
To own what was never mine.

How do I live free in this Black body?
I do not have an answer.
It is 8 a.m. in a foreign country
Where I am a lone stranger floating
On the privilege to flee
If only for a short while
I bask in the ease of escape
Warm my brown, brown skin
Under the glow of a forgetful sun.

Meanwhile, back home,
In the divided house

It becomes increasingly hard to return to,
Another human is disappeared
Burned, choked, gunned down without remorse
In a public square
With footage
With evidence
With proof
Of all the malicious fear
That can lead one human to kill another.
A child, a mother.

With such disrespect for human life
Without repercussion.

I have learned
The law only applies for some
In that rotted system
A cage
Its stench
An overripe, ripe fruit
Black and molded
Aired to the high heavens

I try to escape
The constant reminder of how little my life matters to them
How little my someday children will matter to them
The fear wired into my body from birth

I am reminded daily
Of all the reasons to fear walking in all this Black
Black people are not safe in this country
Extinguished with the brute force of the "law"
In my parents' home,
This blue-bruised, white-picket-fenced-in, bloodred soil,
The only motherland I have ever known,
So many of my people are disappeared.
Robbed so long of real autonomy

There is a tax for being Black in this country
And we are forced to pay,
In blood, in time. They say,
With time . . . it will get better
It never does

All my kin have been writing these poems
Singing these damn songs
We shall overcome . . . some day
That is never today. That has never been tomorrow

And how many of us will have to die
Publicly
Shot down like dogs or lions or gorillas
Or wait, you care about those
Shot down like Black people.
What else can I do but write?

Today I begin to imagine what this body
Glittering in all its Black beauty
Would look like alive and free

I start with laughter,
Dance, song,
Reconnected to the ancestors,
Spirits and tradition
Lost so long ago.

Marriage

Can more of our days be like today?
Soft and sweet
Morning porch sun
Linens and laughter
Cuddles that could last forever
Conversations without our phones
Mofongos down the block
Our mouths hot with garlic
Bellies saturated and full
Decadent and divine
Baby, can we take more days in the sun like this?
Cuddling for hour-long naps that turn to sunsets
Can we skip the show entirely?
Hang back and, dare I say,
Miss out?
Discover this new thing all the kids are talking about
JOMO?
And rediscover each other
Let's laugh on the couch till our cheeks hurt
Seeing our righteous reflections mirrored on television screens
Reconnecting to our hearts
Moonshine and Zion hop up on the couch
Our little fur family snuggled in
Today, this is all that I need right now
This love
This warmth
This home
This space I feel safe
And loved
And happy
Drifting off to blues and jazz standards
Billie and Dinah sing us off to sleep
But before I go,
More of this love,
More forever

Jazz

Once upon a time
The devil had a song so blue
God had to kick him out of heaven.

Let me go out like that,
Raptured in a poem so jazz
Even the gods had to fear me.

Adoration and Song

I found God in a song once
felt my soul
tapping her shoe
middle of church pew
run holyghost
church hat
screaming in the stands
the world makes sense.
my heart made sense.
music helps me find
lost places.

God smiled at me from the belly of a blues song once
low and grumbling like a laughing engine
cigarette smoke and gin
creeping along Her breath
I came alive in the middle of a dark room
found my body bending in ways
impossible
I was red lips
invincible

I lost myself to rhythm once
dove into a trance
took a deep breath of bass
and listened
to the voices pulling apart rib cages
bursting to speak through
thudding against my rib cage.
told my heart to go sit down somewhere

did you know God came to me *a cappella* once?
sang deep from somewhere unknown
reached in
remixed remastered
She sang

a bliss so magic
She made me believe
again.
if only for the moment,
we are one and the same.
this music and me.

floating along our melody
I remembered a part of me
that almost died
She is still alive
still sitting by the fire
waiting for me to kindle her
with adoration and song.

The Roller Rink

heaven is a roller rink playing all my favorite tunes
the dj attuned to the most perfect muse
must be some kind of magic
that brings us all to our feet
to celebrate and savor
this tiny armistice between sob and release
the glide and relief, good god the
joy that sparkles under a righteous disco and flood
lights us through our darkest days
no thief in the night
no sorry sorrow forced upon us
by law, state, or fate
no grief-filled goodbyes
we lift our eyes,
make meaning even in the mourning,
gift ourselves this present
to feel and just skate

maybe, just maybe,
god made the roller rink
so we'd know how to fly,

an exalt and groove
moving toward the kind of jubilee
that lasts, stays, heals, loves,
transforms with every spin, dip, and shake

justice, a melody we make,
the absolute miracle of a record, a life,
a wheel that keeps on spinning

After the Meeting

My sisters fold me in their arms
Circling with comfort and care
I am surrounded by love
They carry me through dark tides
Lift me up
Ask what I need
Show up
With sage and crystals to cleanse the space
Cook food when I don't even know how to answer
They hold me when I feel most
Untethered
Call me back home from shore
This is love in action
Community care in practice
They remind me
I am safe
I am held
I am grateful

Dreams

Dreams are the fragile
Matter that gods are made of
To dream is to God.

Let's Just Say
What shall we build
on the ashes of a nightmare?
—Robin D. G. Kelley

Let's just say when.
When the sun rises again
And the birds call and sing the start of this new day
We have arrived
And when from the rubble of devastation
Instead of fists and fear
This time
Our hands stretch out, one to the other
Let's close open palms 'round open palms and pull each other up and
out

I want only to believe, or
Rather, I know
I know, I know, I know
That this time we hold tight
And refuse to let go
Our arms wrapped around each other
Similar and same sorrow, warm on dusty cheeks
I know when we are there, face to face
Smack in the shock of loss and hurt and the weight of all this heavy
Eye to eye, heart to heart
We will recognize

Tears speak the same language
This life shit is hard
But by some miraculous stroke
Of luck, of wonder, of privilege, of possibility
We are still here with breath left in lungs

To still do something about it

Let's just say the sun has risen, and now
On this new dawn that we've been fighting for

The people have food and song
And somewhere comes the clarion call
Of hope, of chance that THIS time
This time we can actually rebuild
A city where those who hunger can eat
Where those who shiver find shelter
Where those who hurt have healing
Where our children and elders are safe, supported, and held
Where our lives and our bodies are ours
And they matter.

That there too is space for community, care, family, romance, laughter, adventure, rest, play,
the universal needs that keep a community whole

I have to believe in this wide and wondrous world
That on the other end
Of hurt and pain and the kind of sadness
That will fold a body in half
That there too is room for joy
That there too is opportunity
That the heart can burst full of wonder and awe and magic.
That when you hold my hand
That when we are here, heart to heart
On the ashes of decisions not made for, from, or by us
That we can still choose today
That we can still choose each other.

So let's just say
Let's just say out loud
That somehow we make it to morning
When it feels like all we've got is mourning
Let's just say *yes and*
And somehow a seed of a miracle blooms
From that endless, endless ocean of tears
We water something new
And I have to believe that we won't turn our backs on each other
But instead turn toward

Both of us green on the dawn of possibility
That we can still build from that heart-centered place
That knows love, that knows care, compassion
That knows there is still much to be repurposed, reimagined

That not all is lost
That our hearts still feel
All of this
Because even still, dawn breaks, and
Somewhere, a bird sings.

Holding Space for the Black Girls

The ones who feel tomorrow's too much
The ones who couldn't stay
The ones who had to leave
Whose time had run
The ones who were running
Where you goin' so fast, girl?
I see you, sis
Wish these words could have been balm
Enough to keep you safe
Enough to keep you here
I wish you had another sun
Wish this world were not so cold
To girls with skin like ours
I get it
That sharp pain in your chest
The fear of breath
The fear of life
The stress, the trauma, the anxiety
Despite it all
I see you, sis
Even though it's too late
I know you had to jet
Had to fly
I'm so sorry we failed you
Didn't notice sooner
Couldn't stop your crane descent
We all miss you so deep
Cry these nights when you're not here
No matter how well we thought we knew you
Or didn't know
The pain you were hiding
The pain you held so tight
Sis, you were a light
And though history has claimed you back
We light candles in the dark
Remember you in the morning

Your name a holy praise
A sacred reminder
That love is everlasting
This love is everlasting

Determined Energies

Peace to the ones who see me
See me as I truly am
Who believe in me enough
To coax me out of my shell
And breathe into the woman
I was born to be
Peace to the support
For possessing the patience
It sometimes takes
To help tear down these walls I've built around me
For reminding me that no matter how hard I try
There is no hiding from my inner truth
Thank you for helping me find that place
For ignoring the terrified little girl too afraid to confront
The ghosts of demons past
And showing me how to use them more as creative outlet
Than unconfronted fear
Peace for the immeasurable love
It takes to connect with a being
From one human heart to another
I am grateful to learn from you
Grow with you
Peace to our experience
And to the determined energies that
Crossed our paths.

I Believe

I believe in what I feel
Whatever gut or Spirit tells me
I listen
With the intent of a student
Thirsting for wisdom
I believe in love
Emotions are impossible to ignore
I believe there are places
In the human heart
Where there is space enough to forgive
Though I have yet to find it completely
I am still searching with flashlight and key
Ready to unlock the parts of me
That can do the impossible
I believe we are capable
Of wondrous things
I believe
The heart is an expanding chamber,
Where there are many rooms
And the air is clear
Clean
I feel the heart can expand
To absorb the pain
And change it to Light
Here there is room enough for plenty
Our love is immeasurably sacred
We too are sacred
I believe we need to immerse ourselves in everything that
Feels good to Spirit
Listen closely, beloved
There is a voice
A song set in the very
Epicenter of our souls
Quaking to release
Begging to be sung, and
At the risk of everything that matters

Listen
There is a voice that
Must be spoken
Must be validated
Nurtured
Heard
I see you
I hear you
I feel you,
Believe there is power in our collective
Expression is a luxury
That we are wealthy enough to indulge
At long last I can see
There is no me
But I feel we
Are powerful
And beautiful
Surging with so much potential
Sparking electric in our bones
We were built for feeling
Every inch of our humanity
This life experience is every part of the journey
I believe in the journey
In love
In us we must trust
Lest we be swallowed
By those who are not
Brave enough to see
The light and love
I believe
We were born
To feel

This Chapter

I am dedicating this chapter of my life
To chasing joy with abandon
To finding that *je ne sais quoi* that makes
My jaw drop with delight
My heart skip a beat
My feet roll over paths yet undiscovered

This is my gift to me
A chance to pause and reflect
Hold my loved ones tight
Cheers to the pamper

The laughter bubbling from within
My tongue a well of water and savor

Here's to the shared adventure

The wonder poured into cups overflowing
My cup is full and I am grateful.
I find myself floating now
From the westernmost point of the world
To castles in the sky drenched in apricot sunsets

The view is that much better with you here

Let's call this chapter happiness, glee
Blessed and blissful
With this miraculous life I got

I'm tryna live
Fly
Wander
Rejuvenate
The world is full of so many wonders

Lust-drenched sunsets and exhilarations, wishes already come true

Reunions with family from so long ago
See how we stunt?
Take our entire village overseas
And take over entire villages
That ain't never seen so much melanin poppin'

Shining
Our light from shore to shore

There are so many paths I'd like to travel

So many sunrises I've yet to see

So many dance floors I've yet to grace
With my clumsy, my reckless, my off-beat fun

I'm calling this chapter mine
A return to me
I am pouring into myself

Swimming in natural hot springs
My hair drenched in clay

It feels different now
I am not the same

A work of art in the crafting

This be my year of yes, now, why not me?

And damn right, it's a celebration

You don't even know the half
All that I have been through
All that I've survived

Damn right, it's time to dance, frolic, hug, skate
Damn right, this queer Black girl is absolutely living her best life

This life is a grand adventure
And I am here to play

Proclamation (On Loving Myself to Life)

Today I proclaim joy
My laughter too big for its own good
It stretches the insides of my perfect belly
And makes me full
Of love, of light, of freedom
Today I am free to love myself to LIFE!
Authentically. Boldly.
Today I tell myself I am beautiful (and mean it)
Am more than just the physical shell
I am powerful. I speak my truth
Unapologetically.
Sustained by the Spirit of the ancestors
And of those who came before me
I am all the change I was lookin' for
I educate and empower my community
Remembering today how worthy I am of love in every form.
I know I don't say this often enough:
Dear Black girl, sparking with so much magic in your bones
I love you; I am here for you. You are enough.

A Poem for My Girls on a Saturday Night

Tonight the women gathered along the river
Dedicated to care for each other
Learning together in the present
Theorizing a past provided by our elders
Building a future full of affirmations
We are Rising
Tonight the Black women gathered
To speak about the times
To navigate our way through and across trauma
And even still, we make light, find joy
Even at the bottom of an endless stream
Tears flow and water gardens.
And we still come with the new moon and the love from our ancestors.
Been doin' this God work
Since before we even knew
How to put a name to the pain
We unpack a sorrow too familiar
Carrying all this baggage
We let go.
The weight a little easier
To hold with all these brown hands
Letting go
Holding up
Trusting
Each other whole
Braiding, combing, oiling love into locks and fros
Tenderness at the root
There is tenderness in these roots.

And somehow we find a way
To laugh and laugh and laugh
And joy is an old friend
Come over with a bottle of wine (and her stash of curly pudding)
And that new-new playlist
Chock-full'a Erykah Lauryn Jill Jamila Seinabo that young FKA

And a reminder that we matter
Are worthy
Important
And most importantly, loved.
We love.
And somehow find
Hope again, home again
Don't let the hype fool you
Once upon a time,
Black women
Lifted each other up
And we lived, honey. We thrived.

Who Am I

My name is Yazmin Monét Watkins and
I am a human being falling in love with all my flaws
My perfections, I be both affirmation and answer
Full of so many questions
I challenge status quo
Racing 'round intersections
I plan on skidding into the finish line of this honey-sweet life
Giving it all I got
Till the wheel comes off
Its hinge
(Been binge-watchin' *Love Island*, guess I'm into reality too)
A contradiction
Far too clumsy for my own good, tripping and falling into adventures
all across this planet
Southwest tried to get me
I really am tryna get away
I'm low-key/high-key hella corny
Yeah, I grew up off Corning and Slauson and Chariton
Ladera raised me, Granada made me
Spent some suns around La Jolla
I am most at home by the sea
Reconnect to Spirit whenever I'm swimmin'
Floatin' on daydreams
Following passions, attuned to that inner voice that screams YES,
now, why not me?
I be in my feelings.
Workin' on myself every day
Here to claim what I deserve
Chart my future like North Star, remember ancestors got me
I am Leola's great-granddaughter
Got my grandmother's daily word, got her prayers at my back
I be descendant of masterminds from the South, moving westward,
building futures
That they could only dream of
Black feminist thought served at the table they made
Dr. Mom made sure we was eatin'.

I am part of a lineage of powerful Black women conjuring that OG
Black Girl Magic
Manifesting better futures
We have all we need and more
I am the generational curse breaker
The ground shaker, grew up in Cali
What'd you expect but an earthquake?
Set up for success. Yeah, I'm all the way up
I'm a roller, marathon skater,
Run a Boston on that ass
Yeah, I bid whist on occasion,
Come and see me if you dare
I dare to be powerful, shine my light in every room
I was his wife and her partner,
Now I am most my own
I am a cat mom
And a daughter. I'm your sister, I'm your teacher, coolest auntie
(almost) on TikTok
Creating laughter and good cheer everywhere I go

I say I am a Black bisexual poet/screenwriter/actor/comedian/
improviser/producer/teaching artist/more
creating worlds that look like us
So that anyone who hears my voice will see their truth reflected back

#AudreTaughtMe
And even still, I am not my job, not my hair
Not my titles. Not who I've loved. Or where I've gone.
I've done so much and am on the precipice of so much more

I am here to experience all the good life has to offer,
I am here to drink my fill
I am grateful
I am glowing, I am growing
I am enough. I am enough. I am enough.
Right here and right now.
Love myself as I am

I am here and alive
And what a celebration.

Gratitude

I am eternally grateful for the community of love that has brought me safely to shore time and again. I know I don't have enough words, pages, or space to even begin to thank each person who has touched my life, but before they Oscars-music me out of my own acknowledgment section . . .

Thank you to my publisher Andrews McMeel, my editor Danys, and art director Tiffany for your patience and guidance ushering this book into the world. My deepest gratitude to Safia for editing and nurturing this book early on. Many thanks to Lori for this dreamy cover design; I could float and get lost in these waves. Thank you!

To my amazing agent at WME, Haley Heidemann, whose whole-hearted belief in my book and my poetry ensured these words would make it into the hands of those who need it, thank you. I'd also like to extend gratitude to my manager Mike for connecting and helping me grow.

To my parents, Rosalie Dianne Bartlow and Cedric Lee Watkins, thank you for bringing me earth side. I am the woman I am today because of you. Thank you, Mom, for showing me unconditional love in practice. We had fun in this lifetime together. Thank you, Dad, for the gift of gab and gumption and challenging me to always be my truest self. Thank you both for believing in my art and the encouragement to go after my dreams. For pushing me to "keep throwing mud at the wall." It is starting to stick. I will miss you both every day of my life.

I want to acknowledge all my other ancestors rooting for me from the other side. Especially my beloved cousin Tanea Rain Adero, who gave me the gift of journaling early on. That Sanrio stationery was the space for my earliest poems and confessions—I owe you. To my cousin Lillia, the brightest diamond in the sky. I miss you, little cousin, I wish we had more time. Rest easy Grandma Lillie, Grandpa Bartlow, Grandma Mabel, Grandpa Watkins, Uncle Bobby, Aunt Yvonne, Aunt Rosa, Cousin Jamaal, Great- Grandma and Grandpa

Turney, and Great-Grandparents Watkins. Your memories live on. Thank you for the impact you have had in shaping my life.

To my family that is still here, we out here! Thank you for loving me as I am and pouring into me no matter what. I love you Amber, Ced, and Jade. Thank you, Brandon, Channon, and Tim, for loving my siblings so fully. To my beloved nieces and nephews, Paris, Madison, Zoe, August, Miles, Lily, Regan, and Max, I love you all fiercely and will always be here for you. I could not be rooting for you harder. So much love to my elders, Uncle John, Aunt Cathy, Uncle D, Khadija, and Auntie Fundisha, thank you for your love and wisdom. Love to my cousins on both sides, especially Theresa and Emani, I love our poetry nights out.

To Sasha, my love. I am in awe of our connection. It has shifted the very molecules in my body. What a gift, this love. Every present moment has been the honor of my lifetime. I am forever changed.

To David, king of the side eye, thee snarkiest of snark knights, my safe harbor, how grateful I am to learn from your brilliance. I love you. Thank you for all the laughs, understanding, care, and compassion. I hope this conversation never ends. You and Sasha both have held me through the most difficult times. Through the best of times. I would not be here without you. I count my lucky stars to know love in such abundance.

To my people. My frans. The folks who have seen me through the tears, the laugh-out-loud funny, the awkward. I really lucked out in this lifetime. Dominique, Lindsey, Ravaut, Oli, Kyle, Corinne, Audrey, Nina, Shaka, Tabby, Sayo, Anthony, Nozipho, Sharmeen, Chioma, Lauren, Mia, Ari, Jeremy, Bri, Kamry, Rinny, Yadira, Aja, Maya, Lydie, Jonnae, Jake and Sakari, and so many more I don't have enough space to list, your friendship is the boat that steers me back to shore every time. Thank you for holding me through the rain and shine. This life with you makes me so full!

To my Black Lives Matter LA fam, my grassroots peeps, my folks on the front lines, the work you do is literally changing the world. Thank you for your unwavering love and dedication to the liberation of our people. How grateful I am to learn from and organize with you: Melina, Phil, Shelia, Thandiwe, Tabatha, Jan, Mama Paula, Baba Akili, Joseph, Megan and Daniel, Tyler, Liv, Tynacity, Michael, Michael, Kim, Quincy, Verneen, Ashley, Cori, Chris, Kasey, Angela, Stephen, La Mikia, Maraky, Sheila, TK, Richie, Future, Patrisse, Rahje. Amara Kioni, I am so grateful to be your mentor, you inspire me.

White people for Black lives, you give me hope.

I cannot begin to express my gratitude for The Silent Poets. Flow, Rich, Tynesha, Ashley, Tiffany, Tiff Tiff. Y'all were instrumental in helping me find my voice. "We will no longer *be* silent."

To the poets. Tonya, my dear friend, I miss the sound of your voice. Damnyo, Jasmine W., Matty S., Romero, Poetic, Arielle, Fei, Shelley, Cuban, Alyesha, Yesika, Edwin, Mo, Elizabeth, Funmilola, Jasmine M., Selina, Aja, Jamilla, Blake, and the DPL crew, growing in this poetry community with y'all has been such a privilege.

Thank you to every teacher, mentor, and student who has touched my life, especially Dean B., Philogene, and Johnson. Thank you for shaping and molding me.

Love to my Posse family, my Dickinson family, my line sisters, and my sweet Sorors of DST and the Upsilon Delta chapter. Who knew Pennsylvania would bring such incredible people into my life.

Shout out always to my Black Lesbians United family. BLU is such an important space, and I am so very grateful for our community and the invitation to always be myself.

To my therapist Rande, girl, I would not be here without your heart and guidance. Thank you a million times over.

Love to Obama's Other Daughters. To Paul and Lucia and every person who has ever said *yes*. Y'all literally made my TV writing dreams come true.

Thank you to every person who said *no* and led me to this *hell yes* of a life.

There are so many names listed and so many more that I do not have space to name, but for every moment we have shared together, thank you, thank you, thank you.

And last but certainly not least, thank you, dear reader, for holding space for my story. How grateful I am to cross paths with you. May your days be filled with joy and light and love that fills your cup. Wishing you well on your journey.

Oh! And um, gratitude to my cats Moonshine and Zion. You will never read this but thank you for all the wet-nose kisses and cuddles while I wrote these poems. Stop tearing up the carpet! Love you Tigre, for whom I wrote my first poem.

About the Author

Yazmin Monét Watkins is a poet, comedian, writer, actress, educator, and organizer whose body of work weaves art and activism, exploring the intersection of race, gender, sexuality, self-love, and all things Black Girl Magic. Watkins serves as the co-chair of the Arts & Culture committee for Black Lives Matter Los Angeles.

Once, Beyoncé said she liked her hair.